Let's Explore

Sorting and sets

by Henry Pluckrose

W
FRANKLIN WATTS
NEW YORK • LONDON • SYDNEY

Author's note

This book is one of a series which has been designed to encourage young readers to think about the everyday concepts that form part of their world. The text and photographs complement each other, and both elements combine to provide starting points for discussion. Although each book is complete in itself, each title links closely with others in the set, so presenting an ideal platform for learning.

I have consciously avoided 'writing down' to my readers. Young children like to know the 'real' words for things, and are better able to express themselves when they can use correct terms with confidence.

Young children learn from the experiences they share with adults around them. The child offers his or her ideas which are then developed and extended through the adult. The books in this series are a means for the child and adult to share informal talk, photographs and text, and the ideas which accompany them.

One particular element merits comment. Information books are also reading books. Like a successful story book, an effective information book will be turned to again and again. As children develop, their appreciation of the significance of fact develops too. The young child who asks 'What is a number?' may subsequently and more provocatively ask, 'What is the biggest number in the world?' Thoughts take time to generate. Hopefully books like those in this series provide the momentum for this.

Henry Pluckrose

Contents

4

We can group things
in all kinds of ways.
We can group them
by colour, size, shape
or by how they are used.
We call this 'sorting'.

When we group or sort things,
we put them into a set.
A set is a group of things
that are similar in some way.
How are these things similar?

7

When we sort, we look
for things which are the same,
and for things which are different.
What is the same
about these boats?
What is different about them?

9

Sometimes we put things into sets
to make them easier to find.
The greengrocer puts the same
types of vegetables together.
He separates the vegetables
from the fruit.

In a library, the books
are sorted into groups.
Books about similar things
are put together
on the same shelf.

We can sort things by size.
We could sort these dogs
into two sets – one set of adults
and one set of puppies.
How else could
we sort them?

15

16

Sometimes we sort by pattern.

Hattie has lost a sock.

Can you find one to match

the one she is wearing?

We can sort things by shape.
Look at this plate of biscuits.
How many different
shapes can you see?
How could you sort them?

These musical instruments
can be sorted into groups.
Some of the children
are blowing their instruments.
Some of the children
are hitting their instruments.
Can you see another
group of instruments?

A large set can often be sorted into smaller sets. This is a set of toys. Can you put the toys into smaller sets?

This jar is full of different buttons.
Most of the buttons here
could belong to more than one set.

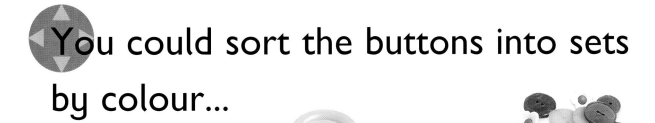 You could sort the buttons into sets by colour...

or by shape...

How else could you sort them?

All the sweets in the red circle are pink.

All the sweets in the blue circle have wrappers.

The sweets that are in both circles are pink and have wrappers.

These sweets belong to both sets.

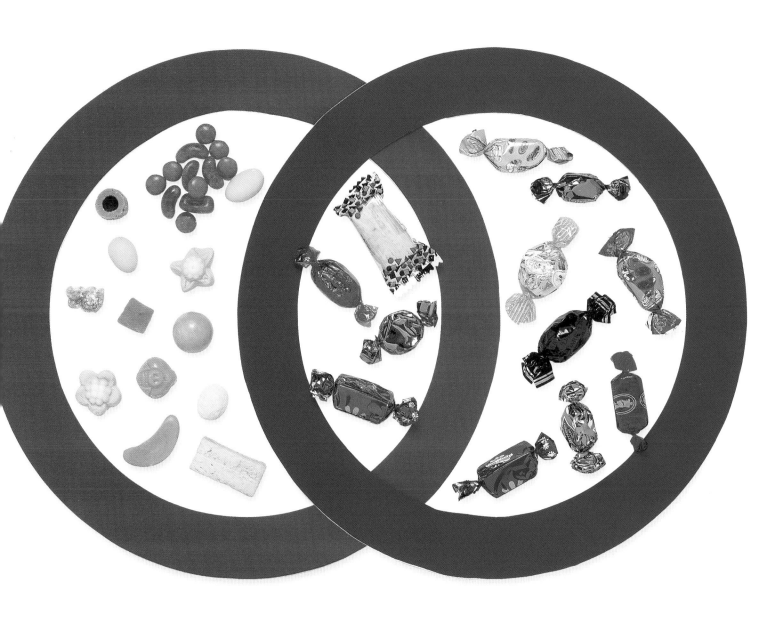

Look at these bunches of flowers.
Which bunch is the odd one out?
How else could the flowers
be sorted?

29

What colours are
the different butterflies?

Are they the same size?

Are they the same shape?

These questions help us to find out
what kind of butterflies they are.

Sorting tells us more
about our world.

Index

First published in 1999 by
Franklin Watts
96 Leonard Street
London
EC2A 4XD

Franklin Watts Australia
14 Mars Road
Lane Cove
NSW 2066

Copyright © Franklin Watts 1999

ISBN 0 7496 3580 0

Dewey Decimal
Classification Number 510

A CIP catalogue record for this book is
available from the British Library

Series editor: Louise John
Series designer: Jason Anscomb
Series consultant: Peter Patilla

Printed in Hong Kong

Picture Credits:
Steve Shott Photography pp. cover and title
page, 4, 5, 7, 8, 9, 16, 18, 19, 20, 23, 24, 25, 27,
28, 29; Bubbles p. 12 (Ian West); Image Bank
pp. 11 (Michael Melford), 31 (Jody Dole);
Tracy Morgan Animal Photography pp. 14,
15.

With thanks to our models:
Reid Burns, Karim Chehab, Alex Dymock,
Danielle Grimmett-Gardiner, Tom Grylls,
Hattie Hundertmark, Charlie Newton and
Laura Wynn.